The 121 Laws for Inner Peace

The 121 Laws for Inner Peace

A Comprehensive Guide to Self-Discovery, Growth, and Harmony

Mela Zenith

To all those seeking inner peace and more fulfilling life, may this book serve as a guiding light on your journey.

With love and gratitude.

CONTENT

Introduction: Finding Inner Peace   3

I.   Cultivating Self-Care and Well-Being   5

II.   Practicing Compassion and Empathy   19

III.   Embracing Personal Growth and Learning   33

IV.   Mastering Communication and Relationships   47

V.   Living Mindfully and Spiritually   61

VI.   Cultivating Gratitude and Appreciation   75

VII.   Serving Others and Making a Difference   89

VIII.   Taking Responsibility and Being Accountable   103

IX.   Achieving Balance and Harmony   117

X.   Embracing Environmental Sustainability   131

XI.   Promoting Social Justice and Equality   145

Reflection: Your Laws for Inner Peace   159

Laws Index   173

Peace begins with a smile.

- Mother Teresa

Finding Inner Peace

Welcome to «121 Laws for Inner Peace», a guidebook for achieving inner harmony and spreading peace in your community and the world. In a time of uncertainty and chaos, this book offers a path towards cultivating compassion, mindfulness, and sustainability.

In this book, you will find 121 laws divided into 11 categories, each focusing on a different aspect of a peaceful and fulfilling life. From self-care and well-being to social justice and equality, these laws provide practical and inspirational guidance to help you live a life of peace.

Whether you are seeking personal growth and spiritual development, or want to create positive change in the world, these laws offer a roadmap towards a more peaceful and harmonious existence. By incorporating these principles into your daily life, you will not only find greater fulfillment and joy, but also contribute to the greater good of all.

This book is not just a personal guide, but also a call to action. By embracing these laws, you have the power to create a ripple effect of peace and compassion, transforming not only yourself, but also the world around you.

So, take a deep breath, open your heart, and embark on a journey towards a life of peace with «121 Laws for Inner Peace.»

I

Self-care and well-being

1. Prioritize rest and sleep

The cornerstone of your well-being and productivity is rooted in sufficient rest and sleep. Allowing your body and mind to recuperate and rejuvenate is key to maintaining optimal health. Sleep is a necessity, not a luxury; ensure you make it a central part of your routine.

2. Find healthy outlets for stress and emotions

Life comes with stress and emotions, but identifying healthy ways to manage them is crucial. This might involve confiding in someone, writing, painting, or engaging in any other activity that brings relaxation and joy. Embracing positive coping techniques can help you navigate stress and emotions effectively.

3. Practice mindfulness and being present in the moment

Adopting mindfulness and being present allows you to fully appreciate life. It enables you to recognize life's beauty and enhance your awareness of your surroundings, thoughts, and emotions. Mindfulness practice cultivates a sense of serenity and fulfillment, leading to a purpose-driven life.

4. Cultivate inner peace and contentment

Nurturing inner peace and contentment helps you find solace and happiness from within, regardless of external factors. Prioritizing self-care and mindfulness can create a deep sense of inner calm and happiness that you can share with others. Through this practice, you establish a life rooted in peace and contentment while building resilience to face adversity.

5. Avoid harmful substances or behaviors

Minimizing or avoiding detrimental substances and behaviors contributes to a healthy and vibrant life. By consciously choosing to distance yourself from things that negatively affect your physical, mental, and emotional health, you cultivate a life full of energy and vitality, self-care, and self-respect, taking charge of your well-being and happiness.

6. Seek professional help when needed

Seeking professional help when needed is a brave and responsible action. It allows you to address your physical and mental health needs and obtain the necessary support to overcome challenges or difficulties. Understand that everyone faces life's hurdles, and seeking assistance demonstrates strength, not weakness. By connecting with professionals, you can gain new insights and tools to navigate tough situations and emotions.

7. Practice self-care regularly

Self-care is the foundation of a balanced and healthy life. By focusing on your physical, emotional, and mental well-being, you can foster resilience and inner strength. Regular self-care practices help manage stress and prevent burnout while promoting a positive self-image and self-esteem. When you care for yourself, you can be more present in relationships and contribute to the world around you with a sense of purpose and fulfillment.

8. Find a form of exercise that you enjoy

Participate in physical exercises that bring happiness and support overall well-being. By finding enjoyable physical activities, you can develop a sense of satisfaction and make them a regular part of your life. Whether it's dancing, hiking, or practicing yoga, allocate time for physical activity to improve your physical, mental, and emotional health. Embrace the benefits of movement and find a sustainable and enjoyable way to stay active.

9. Take care of your mental health

Emphasizing mental health is crucial for experiencing a balanced and fulfilling life. By concentrating on emotional well-being, you can develop resilience, inner strength, and a positive outlook on life. Seek help when needed, engage in self-care, and establish healthy coping strategies to build a life characterized by emotional stability and balance. Your mental health is a valuable asset that should be cherished and protected, allowing you to be your most authentic self in every aspect of life.

10. Practice stress-management techniques

Managing stress effectively is essential for achieving balance and wellness. By incorporating stress-reduction techniques, you can foster a calm and composed demeanor, leading to a life marked by inner harmony and overall well-being. Utilizing methods such as meditation, physical activity, yoga, breathing exercises, or setting aside personal time can enhance stress management, allowing you to better cope with life's challenges and enjoy a more fulfilling, joyful existence.

11. Nurture your creative side

Fostering your creative spirit is an impactful way to explore your inner self and express your unique perspective. Engaging in activities like writing, painting, music, or other artistic expressions can be an essential source of happiness and accomplishment in your life. By dedicating time to nurture your creative talents, you can connect with your deepest passions and create something truly remarkable and meaningful. So, unleash your creativity and cherish the inventive energy within you.

I. Self-care and well-being

If you don't take care of yourself,
you cannot take care of others.

- Dalai Lama

II

Compassion and empathy

12. Be kind to yourself and others

Treating yourself and others with care can transform your life and positively affect those around you. By approaching yourself and others with empathy and understanding, you can nurture inner peace and create a life abundant in positivity and happiness. Release judgment and criticism, practice forgiveness, and establish strong, meaningful relationships. By treating yourself and others kindly, you can unleash a potent force that can inspire and uplift those around you, fostering a world of love and connection.

13. Practice empathy towards others

Empathy is an influential force that enables us to connect deeply with others. By putting ourselves in someone else's position and experiencing their emotions, we can nurture understanding and compassion. Empathy helps us build stronger bonds and create a more harmonious world. Practicing empathy towards others generates a ripple effect of kindness and positivity that can transform our lives and those around us.

14. Cultivate compassion towards yourself and others

Cultivating compassion for yourself and others involves developing a profound sense of empathy and understanding for the human experience. Treating yourself and others gently and graciously creates an environment of acceptance and love. As you practice compassion, you'll uncover a sense of peace and interconnectedness that enriches your life and nourishes your spirit. Compassion allows you to embrace your flaws and those of others, crafting a life abundant in genuine relationships and self-love.

15. Seek to understand before being understood

The capacity to truly listen and grasp another person's viewpoint is an invaluable skill that can lead to deeper connections and more significant interactions. When we strive to comprehend before seeking comprehension, we open ourselves to new ideas and thought processes. Approaching conversations with empathy and a desire to learn fosters connection and understanding, contributing to a world filled with harmony and compassion.

16. Do not judge others based on their beliefs or backgrounds

Respect and accept others for who they are, regardless of their beliefs or backgrounds. Embracing diversity and fostering empathy and compassion creates a life abundant in understanding and harmony. Release the urge to label or categorize others, and approach everyone with an open heart and mind. This way, you can establish meaningful connections and inspire others to follow suit.

17. Value relationships over material possessions

Prioritizing relationships over material goods allows you to emphasize what truly matters in life. Recognizing the significance of meaningful connections with others encourages a sense of love and support, crafting a life abundant in joy and satisfaction. Letting go of the need for material possessions and focusing on relationship-building offers a greater sense of purpose and meaning in your life. This practice promotes generosity, gratitude, and community, extending beyond the scope of material items.

18. Show respect to everyone you encounter

Treat everyone with respect, irrespective of their background or status, to create a world filled with kindness and empathy. By interacting with everyone you encounter with dignity and grace, you foster mutual respect and create a life rich in love and positivity. Remember that each person has a unique story and experiences, and displaying respect contributes to a world that celebrates diversity and inclusivity.

19. Speak up against injustice and oppression

Make your voice heard against injustice and discrimination. Advocating for what is right not only aids those suffering but also nurtures a sense of integrity and authenticity within yourself. By actively supporting marginalized individuals, you can create a ripple effect of positive change and contribute to building a more just and compassionate world. Remember, even small actions can create a significant impact, and your words possess the power to inspire others to act as well.

20. Embrace diversity and differences

Valuing variety and distinctions enables you to cultivate openness and understanding towards others. Acknowledging and appreciating different perspectives, cultures, and beliefs contributes to a more inclusive and harmonious world. Cherishing variety also allows you to broaden your horizons and enrich your life with new experiences and knowledge. By valuing diversity, you can create a world that celebrates each individual's uniqueness, promoting unity and compassion.

21. Practice tolerance and acceptance

Develop an open and accepting mindset by exercising patience towards those who differ from you. By recognizing and respecting the world's diversity, you can encourage unity and understanding. Patience enables you to embrace new perspectives and learn from others, leading to personal growth and a more meaningful life. By practicing acceptance, you can release judgment and criticism, fostering a life filled with love and compassion.

22. Avoid conflict whenever possible

Conflict can be emotionally exhausting and detrimental to all parties involved. By steering clear of conflict when feasible, you can promote a more harmonious and peaceful atmosphere, enabling positive interactions and growth. This can be achieved by practicing active listening, empathy, and striving to understand others' viewpoints. By evading unnecessary conflict, you can create a life abundant in compassion, understanding, and respect.

II. Compassion and empathy

If you want others to be happy, practice compassion.
If you want to be happy, practice compassion.

- Dalai Lama

III

Personal growth and learning

23. Keep an open mind and be willing to learn

Having an open mind and a readiness to learn is vital for personal growth and development. By staying open-minded, you give yourself the chance to explore new ideas and perspectives, resulting in a richer and more satisfying life. Letting go of preconceived ideas and welcoming the unknown might be intimidating, but it's through this vulnerability that we can expand our understanding of the world and ourselves. So, challenge yourself to step out of your comfort zone, be open to new experiences, and see where your journey takes you.

24. Embrace challenges as opportunities for growth

Embracing difficulties with an open and optimistic attitude encourages you to see them as opportunities for personal growth and development. Instead of avoiding challenges, choose to view them as chances for learning and self-improvement. Adopting this approach helps cultivate resilience and determination, allowing you to learn valuable lessons that can help you tackle future obstacles more confidently. By transforming challenges into opportunities for growth, you can create a life full of purpose and meaning.

25. Learn from your mistakes and failures

Use your mistakes and failures as opportunities for growth and self-improvement, rather than dwelling on the past. Approach them with curiosity and an open mind to foster resilience and self-awareness, leading to a life full of progress and success. Remember, it's not about avoiding mistakes but learning from them and moving forward with newfound knowledge and strength.

26. Strive for excellence in all that you do

Pursuing excellence in all you do involves adopting a mindset of continuous improvement and growth. Set high standards for yourself and commit to lifelong learning to unlock your potential and achieve outstanding results. Embrace challenges as growth opportunities and approach each task with purpose and dedication. By embodying a spirit of excellence, you can create a life filled with meaning and accomplishment.

27. Seek feedback and constructive criticism

Embrace growth and improvement opportunities by seeking feedback and constructive criticism from others. Being open to receiving input provides valuable insights and perspectives that can help you grow personally and professionally. Adopting a growth mindset when receiving feedback fosters humility and self-awareness, leading to a life full of progress and development.

28. Pursue your passions and interests

Pursue what you love for a more fulfilling life. Engaging in activities that genuinely interest you helps you find purpose and meaning while allowing you to explore your unique abilities and talents. By following your heart and investing time and energy into what matters to you, you can create a joyful and fulfilling life. Embrace your passions and let them guide you towards a rich and meaningful existence.

29. Set achievable goals and work towards them

Setting attainable goals and working towards them brings purpose and direction to your life. Breaking down larger aspirations into smaller, actionable steps fosters a sense of progress and achievement, leading to a meaningful and fulfilling life. When you set and pursue goals aligned with your values and passions, you can unlock your full potential and inspire others to do the same. So, take the first step towards your dreams today and see where your journey takes you.

30. Expand your knowledge and skills

Seize opportunities to expand your knowledge and abilities to discover your true potential. Continuously seeking new information and experiences cultivates curiosity and growth, leading to a life full of endless possibilities. Whether it's learning a new language, trying a new hobby, or pursuing further education, each step toward self-improvement contributes to a more fulfilling and meaningful life.

31. Practice self-reflection and introspection

Practicing self-reflection and introspection allows you to delve deep into your thoughts, emotions, and actions, helping you become more self-aware and gain a deeper understanding of your strengths, weaknesses, and personal growth opportunities. It enables you to learn from your experiences and make conscious decisions about your presence in the world, leading to a more purposeful and satisfying life.

32. Take calculated risks

Embrace opportunities and take measured risks to unleash your full potential. By stepping out of your comfort zone and facing challenges with a thoughtful and strategic approach, you can foster courage and resilience, and create a life filled with growth and progress. Remember, great achievements rarely come from comfort zones; by taking measured risks, you open yourself up to a world of possibilities and opportunities.

33. Surround yourself with positive influences

Encircle yourself with positive influences and role models to inspire and motivate you to reach your full potential. By connecting with individuals who embody the qualities you admire, you can find a sense of purpose and direction in your own life. Whether it's a mentor, a friend, or a family member, these positive influences can help you stay on track and create a life filled with happiness and fulfillment.

III. Personal growth and learning

*The only true wisdom is in knowing
you know nothing.*

- Socrates

IV

Communication and relationships

34. Practice active listening and effective communication

Effective communication is key for forming significant connections and generating positive change. Active listening is a critical element, enabling you to empathize and respond to others' needs with care and understanding. By practicing meaningful communication, you can establish trust, promote understanding, and create unity in your relationships and communities.

35. Avoid judgment and criticism

By avoiding judgment and criticism, we nurture an atmosphere of empathy and understanding, allowing us to relate to ourselves and others more genuinely, and create a supportive space for growth and healing. Instead of making assumptions or undermining others, approach each situation with an open mind and a warm heart, which will help build deeper connections and a more harmonious world.

36. Practice forgiveness and let go of grudges

Forgiveness is a potent tool for letting go of negativity and moving forward with grace and understanding. By letting go of grudges, you make room for healing and growth. Forgiveness can also strengthen your relationships with others and help you develop empathy and comprehension. Practicing forgiveness liberates you from the weight of anger and resentment, resulting in a life filled with love, peace, and happiness.

37. Find common ground with others

Identifying shared interests with others is a powerful strategy for building bridges and forging connections, even in the face of differing opinions. By actively seeking out common experiences and concentrating on what unites us rather than what separates us, we can foster unity and understanding. This can lead to more profound relationships, increased empathy, and a more fulfilling life. In personal or professional environments, finding shared interests with others is a vital practice for a more harmonious and peaceful world.

38. Let go of the need to be right

Letting go of the need to always be right opens up a world of possibilities and growth. This principle involves relinquishing the urge to always be correct and being open to learning from others. By embracing humility and admitting when we are wrong, we can deepen our connections with those around us and create a collaborative and understanding atmosphere. Letting go of the need to be right liberates us from the pressure of perfectionism and allows us to accept our imperfections with kindness and understanding.

39. Inspire and encourage others

Encouraging and inspiring others is a potent way to generate positive change. By sharing your experiences and insights, you can support those around you and create a ripple effect of positivity. Whether through your words or actions, inspiring others can help them realize their potential and achieve their dreams. Spread positivity and encouragement wherever you go - you never know whose life you might touch and inspire.

40. Build trust and rapport with others

Building trust and rapport with others is vital for developing meaningful relationships. By being consistent and dependable in your interactions, you can nurture trust and respect, creating a life rich in love and connection. Approaching others with sincerity and kindness lays a foundation of mutual understanding and support. Building trust takes time and effort, but the rewards are invaluable, leading to deeper and more rewarding relationships. Whether with family, friends, or colleagues, prioritize trust and rapport in your interactions for a positive impact on all areas of your life.

41. Be honest and transparent in your interactions

Honesty and transparency are essential for forming meaningful relationships. By being authentic and truthful in your interactions, you can foster trust and openness, creating a life filled with genuine connections. Being honest with yourself and others allows you to establish clear boundaries, prevent misunderstandings, and address conflicts in a constructive and respectful manner. It also helps you develop a strong sense of self-worth and self-respect as you live with integrity and honor. Embrace the power of honesty and transparency and watch your relationships and personal growth thrive.

42. Admit when you are wrong and apologize

The ability to admit when you are wrong and offer a heartfelt apology is powerful in building strong relationships. By acknowledging your mistakes and taking responsibility for them, you can demonstrate humility and self-awareness, fostering respect and trust with those around you. Apologizing also indicates that you value others' feelings and perspectives and are committed to making amends. With a willingness to apologize and reconcile, you can nurture a life filled with growth, progress, and positive connections.

43. Seek to understand others' perspectives

Expanding our understanding of the world and those around us requires an open and empathetic mindset. By seeking to comprehend others' perspectives, we can deepen our connections, foster compassion, and promote understanding and unity. Through active listening, thoughtful inquiry, and a willingness to consider different viewpoints, we can broaden our horizons and create a life filled with richness, diversity, and love.

44. Practice non-violent communication

Practicing non-violent communication can transform how you interact with others and foster deeper, more meaningful connections. Instead of responding defensively or aggressively, approach conflict and difficult conversations with empathy and understanding. This allows you to build a sense of connection and resolution, resulting in a life filled with harmony and peace. By using respectful and compassionate language, you can enhance your communication skills and positively impact those around you.

IV. Communication and relationships

The most important thing in communication is to hear what isn't being said.

- Ram Dass

V

Mindfulness and spirituality

45. Cultivate a sense of purpose and meaning

Identifying and nurturing your sense of purpose and significance is crucial for a satisfying and joyful life. Reflect on your values, interests, and passions to discover what genuinely matters to you and gives your life direction and importance. This can help you establish goals and make decisions that align with your purpose, leading to increased fulfillment and satisfaction. With a clear sense of purpose, you can live a life filled with intention, meaning, and experience profound joy and contentment.

46. Practice mindfulness and being in the present moment

Cultivating mindfulness and being present allows you to develop a heightened awareness and appreciation for your surroundings. By focusing on the present moment and savoring each experience, you can nurture gratitude and create a life brimming with presence and joy. Mindfulness helps you slow down, deeply connect with the world, and fully engage with your experiences, providing a greater sense of clarity and focus. It also enables you to release negative thoughts and emotions, instead concentrating on the present moment's beauty and wonder.

47. Connect with nature and the world around you

Immersing yourself in nature and your surroundings enables you to experience awe and wonder at the beauty and intricacy of the natural world. Spending time outdoors, participating in activities like hiking or gardening, or simply observing your environment helps develop appreciation and gratitude for the interconnectedness of all things. This can lead to a deeper understanding of your place in the world and a more profound sense of purpose and meaning in your life.

48. Practice meditation or prayer

Meditate or pray to foster a deeper connection with your inner self and the divine. Setting aside time to quiet your mind and tune into your inner voice can nurture inner peace and clarity. Through this practice, you can gain a more profound understanding of yourself and your surroundings, creating a life filled with purpose and meaning. Whether you choose to meditate, pray, or engage in other forms of contemplative practice, you can access a powerful source of wisdom and insight to guide your journey of self-discovery and spiritual growth.

49. Find spiritual practices that resonate with you

Engage in spiritual practices that align with your core self to find peace, clarity, and a deeper connection to your own spirituality. Whether it's meditation, prayer, mindfulness, or another practice, it's essential to find an approach that aligns with your unique path. Consistently engaging in these practices can foster inner calm, connect with a higher power or the universe, and gain a more in-depth understanding of yourself and your position in the world. Allow these practices to inspire and guide you on your spiritual journey.

50. Practice gratitude and appreciation

Expressing gratitude and appreciation can powerfully transform your perspective on life. Focusing on the positive aspects of your life and giving thanks for them helps develop a sense of contentment and abundance. Cultivate an attitude of gratitude and recognize the blessings in your life, no matter how small they may appear. Approaching life with gratitude opens you up to even more blessings and opportunities for growth and happiness.

51. Foster a sense of connection and community

Nurturing connection and community allows you to establish a supportive network of like-minded individuals who share your values and beliefs. By building meaningful connections and fostering relationships, you can develop a sense of belonging and purpose, creating a life filled with joy and fulfillment. Emphasize the importance of finding your tribe and being part of something more significant than yourself. By working together towards a shared goal, you can create positive change and impact the world.

52. Practice self-reflection and introspection

Self-reflection and introspection are potent tools for personal growth and development. Examining your thoughts, emotions, and actions helps gain a deeper understanding of yourself and your place in the world. This practice fosters mindfulness and self-awareness, enabling you to make more intentional choices and create a life aligned with your values and aspirations. Through self-reflection and introspection, you can access your inner wisdom and creativity, finding clarity and purpose on your journey towards inner peace and fulfillment.

53. Let go of attachments and desires

Embracing detachment leads to inner freedom and peace. By releasing attachments and desires, you can develop a sense of detachment from material possessions and external circumstances. This can lead to a deeper understanding of yourself and the world around you, and a sense of inner fulfillment that is not dependent on external factors. Letting go of attachments can be challenging, but it is a powerful tool for personal growth and transformation. By practicing detachment, you can live a life free from the burden of materialism and find true contentment and joy.

54. Find inner peace and contentment

Uncovering inner peace and satisfaction is a transformative journey, allowing you to nurture harmony and tranquility within yourself. By exploring your inner world and gaining a deeper understanding of your thoughts and emotions, you can learn to navigate life's challenges with greater ease and grace. Practices such as mindfulness, meditation, and self-reflection help you develop a more grounded and centered approach to life, creating a sense of inner peace that permeates every aspect of your being.

55. Live in harmony with yourself and the world around you

Harmonizing with yourself and your surroundings involves cultivating a profound sense of inner peace and balance. Aligning your thoughts, actions, and values with life's natural rhythms allows you to create a life filled with purpose and meaning. When you live in harmony with yourself, you radiate positivity and attract abundance into your life. Embrace the beauty of the present moment and find joy in the simple things, creating a life full of peace, fulfillment, and connection.

V. Mindfulness and spirituality

In the present moment, there is limitless potential.

- Pema Chödrön

VI

Gratitude and appreciation

56. Practice gratitude regularly

Develop a sense of appreciation for life's blessings by regularly practicing gratitude. By recognizing the abundance and goodness around you, you can nurture a feeling of contentment and fulfillment. Focusing on the positive attracts even more positivity, creating a life filled with joy and abundance.

57. Express appreciation to others

Demonstrating appreciation to others helps to deepen the sense of connection and gratitude in your life. By recognizing and thanking those around you for their contributions, you can create a supportive and uplifting environment that encourages growth and positivity. This principle advises you to be kind and compassionate toward others, acknowledging the good in your life. Through expressing appreciation, you can foster a feeling of abundance and fulfillment, building a life full of joy and love.

58. Focus on the positives in your life

Rather than dwelling on life's negative aspects, concentrate on the positives. Cultivating a sense of gratitude and joy by intentionally seeking out the positive aspects of your life, regardless of how small, is encouraged by this principle. Making positivity a habit leads to a more fulfilling and joyful life.

59. Cultivate an attitude of gratitude

Uncover beauty and happiness in life's little moments with this powerful principle. By appreciating simplicity and finding joy in small things, you can nurture a sense of gratitude and appreciation for the world around you. Slow down, savor each experience, and find happiness in the present moment. This principle helps create a life filled with joy and contentment, discovering peace in everyday life's simple pleasures.

60. Cultivate a positive mindset

Adopting an abundance mindset is a transformative practice leading to a life of fulfillment and joy. Shift your focus to the abundance surrounding you rather than lack or scarcity, cultivating a sense of gratitude and appreciation for all life offers. This mindset allows you to approach challenges with optimism and resilience, knowing you have an abundance of resources and support. With an abundance mindset, you can create a life filled with limitless potential and possibilities.

61. Find joy in the simple things

Find contentment and gratitude by appreciating life's little moments. Instead of constantly seeking grandeur and extravagance, discover beauty and fulfillment in the ordinary. Cultivating a mindset of simplicity and mindfulness results in a life full of joy and wonder.

62. Keep a gratitude journal

Gratitude is essential for a fulfilling life. A gratitude journal helps cultivate appreciation for life's blessings. By focusing on the good, regardless of size, you can shift your perspective toward positivity and create a life filled with joy and abundance. This practice helps maintain gratitude even during difficult times, serving as a powerful tool for personal growth and self-care.

63. Share your gratitude with others

Sharing gratitude and appreciation with others not only deepens connections but also nurtures a positive and joyful mindset. Creating a ripple effect of kindness and positivity that extends far beyond yourself is possible by sharing your gratitude with others. It's a powerful reminder that even amid life's challenges, there's always something to be thankful for. Take a moment to express your gratitude and witness how it transforms your relationships and life.

64. Use setbacks and challenges as opportunities for growth

Welcome setbacks and challenges as chances for growth and gratitude. Instead of seeing obstacles as roadblocks, consider them stepping stones toward personal development and self-discovery. Shifting your perspective and finding gratitude amidst adversity cultivates resilience and strength, creating a life filled with purpose and meaning. Remember, every setback offers an opportunity to learn and grow, and every challenge is an occasion to become a better version of yourself.

65. Look for the good in difficult situations

Embrace life's obstacles by identifying the potential growth and learning opportunities within them. Instead of focusing on the negative aspects of tough situations, concentrate on the bright side and discover hidden gems. By adopting an optimistic and resilient mindset, you can turn adversity into a driving force for personal and spiritual development, ultimately creating a life rich in meaning and purpose.

66. Practice generosity and giving to others

Being generous and giving to others helps cultivate a sense of abundance and selflessness. Sharing your resources, time, and talents with others creates a ripple effect of kindness and positivity. This principle encourages you to find joy in giving, whether through small acts of kindness or grand gestures, and to cultivate a sense of gratitude for the abundance in your life.

VI. Gratitude and appreciation

Let us rise up and be thankful, for if we didn't learn a lot today,

at least we learned a little, and if we didn't learn a little,

at least we didn't get sick, and if we got sick,

at least we didn't die; so, let us all be thankful.

\- Buddha

VII

Service and contribution

67. Find ways to give back to your community

Discover ways to contribute to your community and improve the lives of those nearby. Volunteering, supporting a cause you are passionate about, or assisting those in need are all ways to bring meaning and satisfaction to your life. Contributing not only positively impacts your community but also strengthens your sense of purpose and connection.

68. Volunteer your time and resources to a good cause

Committing your time and resources to worthwhile causes is a valuable way to give back and create a positive change. By sharing your talents and resources with causes that matter to you, you can foster a sense of accomplishment and create a life filled with significant experiences and relationships. Whether volunteering locally, participating in community projects, or supporting a nonprofit, your efforts can improve the lives of others and your surroundings.

69. Practice random acts of kindness

Cultivate compassion and spread happiness by performing acts of kindness. These simple, yet impactful gestures can profoundly affect others and the world. Kindness not only brightens someone's day but also fosters empathy and connection. Small acts, like buying coffee for a stranger or helping a neighbor, can create far-reaching positivity. Make kindness a daily habit and witness its transformative power in your life and the lives of others.

70. Use your skills and talents to help others

Use your unique abilities to make a positive impact. By sharing your gifts, you can initiate meaningful change and develop a sense of purpose. Volunteering or employing your professional expertise to help others allows you to make a difference and experience the joy that comes from giving.

71. Be a positive influence on those around you

Encourage positive change by exuding kindness and positivity. Your optimistic demeanor can greatly influence those around you, sparking a chain reaction of goodness. By actively choosing to be a positive force, you can motivate others to adopt a similar mindset, fostering a supportive and uplifting environment. Your actions and words have the power to make a difference.

72. Make a difference in someone's life

Act as a driving force for constructive change by exuding positivity and warmth towards those surrounding you. Your optimistic demeanor and approach can significantly influence the people in your life, generating a chain reaction of benevolence. By deliberately deciding to be a positive presence, you can encourage others to embrace a similar mentality, fostering an environment of encouragement and development. It is through our actions and language that we can embody the transformation we desire in the world.

73. Support charities and organizations

Support organizations that reflect your values, and become an agent of positive change. Contributing your time, resources, or talents helps make a lasting difference and spreads generosity and kindness. Whether local or global, each act of compassion contributes to a brighter future. Find organizations that resonate with your values and support them in a way that feels genuine and meaningful.

74. Practice generosity and giving

Embracing giving and generosity adds meaning and purpose to your life. Acts of kindness and support positively affect those around you. Cultivate an attitude of generosity, making it a habit to bring joy and purpose to your life. Volunteering, donating, or simply showing kindness to others are all ways to practice generosity.

75. Find meaning through service to others

Experience the fulfillment of serving others and find your sense of purpose. Giving back to your community and assisting those in need fosters a deep sense of connection and gratitude. Acts of service, whether through volunteering, donating, or offering support, can bring meaning and happiness to your life.

76. Look for the good in difficult situations

Contribute to a better world by embodying the values and qualities you want to see in others. By doing so, you create a ripple effect of positive change extending beyond yourself. Take responsibility for your actions and their impact, making conscious choices that benefit others and the world at large.

77. Foster a sense of connection and community through service

Cultivating connection and community through service deepens your understanding and appreciation of those around you. Serving others with kindness and empathy creates unity and belonging, fostering meaningful relationships within your community. By contributing to the well-being of others, you can lead a life filled with purpose and positively impact the world around you.

VII. Service and contribution

The best way to find yourself is to lose yourself in the service of others.

- Mahatma Gandhi

VIII

Responsibility and accountability

78. Make ethical and responsible choices

Choose to live a life grounded in ethics by making mindful and responsible decisions that align with your values and principles. Consciously act in ways that foster equity, empathy, and respect for all, crafting a purpose-driven and significant life. Understand the consequences of your choices on yourself, others, and the environment, and strive to make decisions reflecting your highest ideals. With every thoughtful choice, you can positively shape your life and the world.

79. Seek feedback and constructive criticism

Welcome personal growth and improvement by embracing feedback and constructive input from those around you. Instead of fearing criticism, view it as a chance for learning and self-reflection. By considering diverse viewpoints, you can gain valuable insights and deepen your understanding of yourself and the world. With this approach, you can foster openness and humility, creating a life filled with ongoing growth and development.

80. Hold yourself to high standards of integrity and honesty

Become a person of integrity and honesty, holding yourself to high standards of conduct. By living with integrity, you can foster trust and respect in your relationships, creating a life filled with authenticity and purpose. Allow your actions to be guided by your values, and aim to make decisions in line with your ethical compass. Upholding integrity and honesty can lead to a truly satisfying and meaningful life.

81. Take ownership of your life and your choices

Taking ownership of your life and choices empowers you to create your desired reality. Accept responsibility for your decisions, actions, and outcomes instead of blaming external circumstances. When you take control of your life, you can better create a path towards personal growth, success, and fulfillment. This principle encourages you to step into your power and become the master of your own destiny.

82. Avoid blaming others for your problems or mistakes

Accept responsibility for your actions and decisions rather than blaming others for your problems or mistakes. This fosters a sense of accountability and self-awareness, creating a life filled with growth and progress. Recognize that every mistake or setback is an opportunity for learning and improvement, and approach challenges with curiosity and openness. Practice self-reflection and introspection to become a better version of yourself and create a life filled with positivity and achievement.

83. Learn from criticism and use it to improve

Embrace personal refinement through constructive feedback. Learning from criticism is essential for personal growth. By being open to receiving feedback and using it as a tool for improvement, you can cultivate self-awareness and become the best version of yourself. Rather than reacting defensively or dismissively, see criticism as a growth opportunity and use it to polish your skills, attitudes, and behaviors. In doing so, you can reach new levels of success and fulfillment in all areas of your life.

84. Recognize the impact of your actions on others

Recognizing the consequences of your actions on others involves taking responsibility for your behavior and its outcomes. Becoming aware of how your actions impact those around you allows you to make more considerate and intentional choices, leading to greater empathy and understanding in your interactions.

85. Be proactive in solving problems and conflicts

Take the lead in resolving problems and conflicts in your life. By proactively identifying and tackling issues, you can foster a sense of responsibility and empowerment, creating a life filled with progress and growth. Embrace a problem-solving mindset and take necessary steps to create positive change. With determination and resilience, you can overcome any obstacle and achieve your goals.

86. Be accountable to yourself and others

Being responsible to yourself and others means taking accountability for your actions and decisions. It demands honesty, integrity, and admitting to mistakes. By being responsible, you can build trust and respect with others, creating a life of integrity and authenticity. When you hold yourself responsible, you set a positive example for others and inspire them to follow suit. Taking ownership of your actions helps you learn from mistakes and grow as a person.

87. Keep your commitments and promises

Upholding your commitments and promises is essential for establishing trust and respect in your relationships. By following through on your promises, you show your reliability and responsibility, creating a sense of dependability that others can rely on. This not only strengthens your personal relationships but also instills a sense of integrity and self-discipline within yourself.

88. Strive to be a good role model for others

Displaying an exemplary lifestyle and character can inspire others to strive for the best version of themselves. By being a positive example, you can create a meaningful impact on the lives of those around you, uplifting and inspiring them to become better individuals. Strive to embody the values and principles you believe in, letting your actions speak louder than your words. Be mindful of how your behavior may affect others, and aim to be the best version of yourself every day.

VIII. Responsibility and accountability

Freedom and responsibility go hand in hand.
Without responsibility, freedom is a dangerous thing.

- Sri Sri Ravi Shankar

IX

Balance and harmony

89. Practice balance in all areas of your life

Striving for balance in all areas of your life is crucial for a healthy and fulfilling existence. By prioritizing balance, you can cultivate a sense of harmony and avoid the negative effects of excess in any one area. Take a holistic approach to your life, and prioritize the important areas such as your physical health, emotional well-being, personal growth, and relationships. By practicing balance, you can create a life that is grounded, purposeful, and joyous.

90. Prioritize your physical, emotional, and mental well-being

Prioritizing your physical, emotional, and mental well-being is essential for leading a fulfilling and balanced life. By making your health a top priority, you are able to cultivate a sense of inner strength and resilience that will allow you to navigate life's challenges with grace and ease. By taking care of yourself physically through exercise and healthy eating, emotionally through self-care practices and mindfulness, and mentally through practices such as meditation and self-reflection, you are able to create a foundation for a life that is filled with vitality and joy.

91. Set realistic expectations for yourself

Setting realistic expectations for yourself allows you to approach challenges and goals with a healthy and balanced mindset. By being honest with yourself about your abilities and limitations, you can cultivate a sense of self-awareness and avoid undue stress and anxiety. When you set realistic expectations, you can also create a sense of accomplishment and satisfaction as you achieve your goals.

92. Practice time-management and prioritize your time effectively

Prioritize your time effectively and manage it wisely, as time is the most valuable and limited resource we have. By learning to prioritize and focus on what truly matters, you can increase productivity and achieve your goals with greater ease. Through effective time-management, you can reduce stress, improve work-life balance, and create a life that is filled with meaning.

93. Find a healthy work-life balance

Achieving a healthy work-life balance is essential to creating a life of purpose and fulfillment. By setting clear boundaries and prioritizing your time, you can create a sense of harmony and balance between your personal and professional life. This law encourages you to nurture your own well-being and happiness, so that you can show up fully for both yourself and those around you. Striving for a healthy work-life balance allows you to live a life that is filled with joy, meaning, and contentment.

94. Create a positive and peaceful living environment

Creating a positive and peaceful living environment is essential for your well-being and that of those around you. By surrounding yourself with positive energy and creating a space that reflects your values and desires, you can cultivate a sense of calm and harmony. Your environment can impact your mood and behavior, and a peaceful living space can help you feel more centered and relaxed. By taking steps to create a positive and peaceful living environment, you can improve your quality of life and create a space that supports your physical, emotional, and spiritual well-being.

95. Nurture positive relationships and connections

To nurture positive relationships and connections means to invest in the people around you and create a supportive community. By fostering a sense of trust and respect, you can build meaningful relationships and create a network of support that can help you navigate life's challenges. Whether it's through acts of kindness or simply being present for those in your life, nurturing positive connections can lead to a life of love and happiness.

96. Practice moderation in all areas of your life

By practicing moderation in all areas of your life, you can cultivate a sense of balance and harmony. By avoiding excess and finding a healthy middle ground, you can create a life that is filled with simplicity and contentment. Finding the sweet spot between indulgence and abstinence in all aspects of life - be it food, work or entertainment - can help you to live a more mindful and fulfilling existence.

97. Take breaks and practice self-care regularly

Taking regular breaks and practicing self-care is essential for maintaining a healthy and balanced life. By prioritizing your physical, emotional, and mental well-being, you can recharge your batteries and increase your productivity, creativity, and overall satisfaction. Making time for rest, relaxation, and activities that bring you joy and peace can help you find harmony in all areas of your life. Remember, self-care isn't selfish, it's necessary.

98. Find a sense of harmony and balance within yourself

Finding a sense of harmony and balance within yourself and your life allows you to live a life that is centered and grounded. By cultivating a sense of inner peace and equilibrium, you can navigate life's challenges with ease and grace, and create a life that is filled with purpose and joy.

99. Practice simplicity and minimalism

Living a simple and minimalist lifestyle can lead to a greater sense of clarity and inner peace. By practicing simplicity, you can eliminate distractions and focus on what truly matters, allowing you to live a more intentional and fulfilling life. Letting go of excess can also lead to a greater sense of gratitude and appreciation for what you do have. By embracing simplicity, you can create more space for joy, creativity, and connection in your life.

IX. Balance and harmony

*The rhythm of life is a balance
between rest and movement.*

- Osho

X

Environmental sustainability

100. Reduce, reuse, and recycle

Adopting a sustainable lifestyle is crucial in today's world, and practicing the three Rs is one of the most effective ways to do so. By consuming less, repurposing items, and recycling when appropriate, we can significantly lower our carbon footprint and protect the planet for future generations. Small, daily decisions contribute to a more sustainable, harmonious world.

101. Use sustainable products and services

Support sustainable living by selecting environmentally-friendly products and services that minimize environmental harm. By considering the impact our choices have on the planet, we can foster a sense of accountability and respect for Earth, leading to a life rooted in sustainability and balance.

102. Support environmentally-friendly policies and practices

Harmonize with the Earth by conserving essential resources like energy and water. Mindful consumption and waste reduction help lessen your environmental impact and contribute to a sustainable future for all. Adopt small but meaningful steps towards a greener lifestyle, fostering a sense of responsibility and care for our planet, such as turning off lights and electronics when not in use, taking shorter showers, and utilizing public transportation or carpooling to reduce your carbon footprint.

X. Environmental sustainability

103. Advocate for environmental protection

Endorsing environmentally-friendly policies and practices is vital for a sustainable future. By actively supporting policies that encourage ecological balance and reducing our carbon footprint, we can create a healthier planet for ourselves and future generations. This law urges us to be responsible environmental guardians and acknowledge our role in conserving the natural world.

104. Practice responsible tourism and travel

Prioritize environmental preservation and advocate for its protection, as it is essential for the health and sustainability of our planet. By raising awareness and supporting policies and initiatives safeguarding natural resources, you can foster a sense of responsibility and stewardship for the Earth.

105. Learn about environmental issues and their impact

Engage in mindful exploration by practicing responsible tourism and travel. Through careful choices during your journeys, you can minimize your impact on the environment and local communities while encouraging sustainable and ethical practices. Take the time to understand the cultures and customs of the places you visit and support local businesses and initiatives. Responsible tourism and travel enable meaningful and positive experiences for both yourself and the world around you.

106. Learn about environmental issues and their impact

Delve into the intricacies of environmental issues and their consequences on our planet by learning and staying informed. Enhancing your knowledge allows you to make informed decisions that align with your values and contribute to a more sustainable future. By acknowledging your role in the ecosystem, you can foster a sense of stewardship and create a life filled with purpose and impact.

107. Reduce your carbon footprint

Live eco-consciously by reducing your carbon footprint. Through mindful choices regarding transportation, energy use, and waste generation, you can positively impact the environment. By living sustainably, using renewable energy sources, consuming a plant-based diet, and limiting single-use plastics, you foster a sense of responsibility and stewardship for the planet, creating a life in harmony with nature.

108. Support sustainable agriculture and farming practices

Backing sustainable agriculture and farming practices benefits the environment, our health, and the economy. By choosing sustainably grown and produced items, we can support local farmers and communities, lower our carbon footprint, and enhance our well-being as well as the planet's. Embracing sustainable agriculture is an influential way to generate positive change and establish a more resilient and harmonious world for future generations.

109. Foster a sense of connection towards the environment

Develop a connection and sense of accountability towards the environment by adopting sustainable practices and acknowledging the interdependence of all living beings. By treating the environment with care and respect, we can create a healthier and more balanced world for ourselves and future generations. Through mindful action and awareness, we can foster a sense of connection and gratitude for the natural world and its beauty.

110. Encourage environmentally conscious choices

Be a role model and motivate others to make sustainable decisions in their daily lives. By collaborating, we can positively impact the environment and create a more sustainable future for all.

X. Environmental sustainability

The earth provides enough to satisfy every man's needs, but not every man's greed.

- Mahatma Gandhi

XI

Social justice and equality

111. Stand up against discrimination and oppression

By opposing prejudice and mistreatment, you defend not only the rights of others but also uphold your own values and beliefs. Confront those who attempt to harm or separate people based on their race, gender, sexuality, religion, or any other characteristic. Speak out against injustice while promoting fairness and inclusiveness, contributing to a kinder and more equitable world. Our collective efforts can bring about positive change and a more united, just society.

112. Support social justice and equality

Supporting fairness and equal rights means actively working towards a world where everyone is treated justly and respectfully. By acknowledging and challenging oppressive systems, you can help create a more just and equal society. Advocacy, education, or direct action, every effort contributes to building a world where everyone has an equal chance to succeed. Join the movement for fairness and equal rights and be a part of positive change.

113. Recognize and challenge privilege and bias

Be conscious of your own privilege and biases and challenge them in yourself and others. Analyze your beliefs and assumptions to expose any hidden prejudices or privileges that may influence your interactions. By acknowledging and confronting biases, you can foster empathy and understanding, and contribute to a more just and equitable world. Through purposeful actions and reflection, work towards dismantling oppressive systems and promoting inclusiveness and equality.

114. Empower marginalized and underrepresented communities

Empowering disenfranchised and underrepresented groups paves the way for a more fair and just society. By working to elevate those historically excluded from opportunities and resources, we can foster inclusion and belonging for all. Through education, advocacy, and action, we can create a world that appreciates and respects every individual's unique experiences and perspectives, leading a life filled with purpose and impact.

115. Educate yourself and others on social justice issues

Becoming informed about fairness issues is crucial for creating a more just and equitable world. By pursuing information and knowledge on complex social and political matters affecting our communities, we can better understand the root causes of injustice and work towards creating meaningful change. Educating ourselves and others empowers us to act, advocate for marginalized individuals, and establish an inclusive and fair society for all.

116. Eliminate inequalities through collective action

Act collectively to remove systemic obstacles and disparities. By joining forces, you can create a powerful force for change and work towards a more just and equitable world. Together, identify and tackle issues of discrimination and inequality, fostering a more inclusive and equal society for all. Through collective action, contribute to a brighter, more equal future for everyone.

117. Support organizations that promote equality and justice

Supporting organizations that champion justice and equality allows you to actively contribute to positive change. By dedicating time and resources to those working towards a fairer society, you can cultivate a sense of purpose and fulfillment. Supporting these initiatives helps create a more inclusive and compassionate world, moving us closer to a more harmonious future.

118. Practice inclusivity in all areas of your life

Foster inclusiveness and diversity in all aspects of your life. By appreciating differences and promoting equal opportunities, you can create a world filled with respect and unity. In your personal relationships, work, or community, practicing inclusiveness and diversity leads to a more rewarding and enriched life for all. Let go of judgment and bias, and strive to create an atmosphere of acceptance and openness.

119. Use your voice to create positive change

Utilizing your voice and actions can drive positive change. By being deliberate with your words and actions, you can generate a ripple effect of kindness, compassion, and justice. Whether it's standing up for what's right, volunteering your time and resources, or making small daily changes, you have the power to make a difference. Embrace your agency and work towards creating a world filled with love, equality, and sustainability.

120. Find common ground and mutual understanding

Identifying common ground and fostering mutual understanding and respect is crucial for building positive and meaningful relationships with others. By seeking shared values and perspectives, we can build bridges and create unity, even when faced with differences. Approach interactions with empathy and an open mind, and actively work towards resolving conflicts and constructing a more harmonious world.

121. Support sustainable agriculture and farming practices

Championing human rights is essential for creating a just and equitable society. By standing up for the rights of others, you can help ensure that everyone is treated with dignity and respect. Through your actions and advocacy, you can help create a world where everyone is valued and able to live their lives to the fullest. By being a voice for those who are marginalized or oppressed, you can make a difference and create a brighter future for all.

XI. Social justice and equality

Our prime purpose in this life is to help others.
And if you can't help them, at least don't hurt them.

- Dalai Lama

XII

Reflection:
Your Laws for Inner Peace

Reflection:
Your Laws for Inner Peace

This section provides space for you to reflect on their your experiences and perspectives, and to create their own laws for inner peace. Within this space, you will discover prompts and room to record your individual reflections, observations, and realizations.

The intention is to encourage you to nurture your unique path of personal development and the pursuit of inner peace.

Use this section to:

- Reflect on your own values and beliefs.
- Explore your own thoughts and emotions.
- Identify areas for personal growth and development.
- Set achievable goals for yourself.
- Write down your own personal affirmations.
- Develop your own practices for mindfulness and inner peace.

Reflection: Your Laws for Inner Peace

The 121 Laws for Inner Peace

Reflection: Your Laws for Inner Peace

The 121 Laws for Inner Peace

Reflection: Your Laws for Inner Peace

The 121 Laws for Inner Peace

Reflection: Your Laws for Inner Peace

The 121 Laws for Inner Peace

Reflection: Your Laws for Inner Peace

The 121 Laws for Inner Peace

Reflection: Your Laws for Inner Peace

LAWS INDEX

I. Self-care and well-being
1. Prioritize rest and sleep
2. Find healthy outlets for stress and emotions
3. Practice mindfulness and being present in the moment
4. Cultivate inner peace and contentment
5. Avoid harmful substances or behaviors
6. Seek professional help when needed
7. Practice self-care regularly
8. Find a form of exercise that you enjoy
9. Take care of your mental health
10. Practice stress-management techniques
11. Nurture your creative side

II. Compassion and empathy
12. Be kind to yourself and others
13. Practice empathy towards others
14. Cultivate compassion towards yourself and others
15. Seek to understand before being understood
16. Do not judge others based on their beliefs or backgrounds
17. Value relationships over material possessions
18. Show respect to everyone you encounter
19. Speak up against injustice and oppression
20. Embrace diversity and differences
21. Practice tolerance and acceptance
22. Avoid conflict whenever possible

III. Personal growth and learning
23. Keep an open mind and be willing to learn
24. Embrace challenges as opportunities for growth
25. Learn from your mistakes and failures
26. Strive for excellence in all that you do
27. Seek feedback and constructive criticism
28. Pursue your passions and interests
29. Set achievable goals and work towards them
30. Expand your knowledge and skills
31. Practice self-reflection and introspection
32. Take calculated risks
33. Surround yourself with positive influences

IV. Communication and relationships
34. Practice active listening and effective communication
35. Avoid judgment and criticism
36. Practice forgiveness and let go of grudges
37. Find common ground with others
38. Let go of the need to be right
39. Inspire and encourage others
40. Build trust and rapport with others
41. Be honest and transparent in your interactions
42. Admit when you are wrong and apologize
43. Seek to understand others' perspectives
44. Practice non-violent communication

Index

V. Mindfulness and spirituality

45. Cultivate a sense of purpose and meaning
46. Practice mindfulness and being present in the moment
47. Connect with nature and the world around you
48. Practice meditation or prayer
49. Find spiritual practices that resonate with you
50. Practice gratitude and appreciation
51. Foster a sense of connection and community
52. Practice self-reflection and introspection
53. Let go of attachments and desires
54. Find inner peace and contentment
55. Live in harmony with yourself and the world around you

VI. Gratitude and appreciation

56. Practice gratitude regularly
57. Express appreciation to others
58. Focus on the positives in your life
59. Cultivate an attitude of gratitude
60. Cultivate a positive mindset
61. Find joy in the simple things
62. Keep a gratitude journal
63. Share your gratitude with others
64. Use setbacks as opportunities for growth and gratitude
65. Look for the good in difficult situations
66. Practice generosity and giving to others

VII. Service and contribution

67. Find ways to give back to your community
68. Volunteer your time and resources to a good cause
69. Practice random acts of kindness
70. Use your skills and talents to help others
71. Be a positive influence on those around you
72. Make a difference in someone's life
73. Support charities and organizations that align with your values
74. Practice generosity and giving
75. Find meaning and fulfillment through service to others
76. Create positive change in the world
77. Foster a sense of connection and community through service

VIII. Responsibility and accountability

78. Make ethical and responsible choices
79. Seek feedback and constructive criticism
80. Hold yourself to high standards of integrity and honesty
81. Take ownership of your life and your choices
82. Avoid blaming others for your problems or mistakes
83. Learn from criticism and use it to improve
84. Recognize the impact of your actions on others
85. Be proactive in solving problems and conflicts
86. Be accountable to yourself and others
87. Keep your commitments and promises
88. Strive to be a good role model for others

Index

IX. Balance and harmony

89. Practice balance in all areas of your life
90. Prioritize your physical, emotional, and mental well-being
91. Set realistic expectations for yourself
92. Practice time-management and prioritize your time effectively
93. Find a healthy work-life balance
94. Create a positive and peaceful living environment
95. Nurture positive relationships and connections
96. Practice moderation in all areas of your life
97. Take breaks and practice self-care regularly
98. Find a sense of harmony and balance within yourself and your life
99. Practice simplicity and minimalism

X. Environmental sustainability

100. Reduce, reuse, and recycle
101. Use sustainable products and services
102. Conserve energy and water
103. Support environmentally-friendly policies and practices
104. Advocate for environmental protection
105. Practice responsible tourism and travel
106. Learn about environmental issues and their impact
107. Reduce your carbon footprint
108. Support sustainable agriculture and farming practices
109. Foster a sense of connectiontowards the environment
110. Encourage others to make environmentally-conscious choices

XI. Social justice and equality

111. Stand up against discrimination and oppression
112. Support social justice and equality
113. Recognize and challenge privilege and bias
114. Empower marginalized and underrepresented communities
115. Educate yourself and others on social justice issues
116. Eliminate inequalities through collective action
117. Support charities and organizations that promote equality and justice
118. Practice diversity and inclusivity in all areas of your life
119. Use your voice to create positive change in the world
120. Find common ground and mutual understanding
121. Advocate for human rights

Printed in Great Britain
by Amazon

92d42e50-aee2-4414-98ca-dd3637c1fc38R03